Journey Along a River

The Yangtze

Jen Green

WAYLAND

This book is a differentiated text version of *A River Journey The Yangtze* by Rob Bowden.

This edition first published in 2009 by Wayland
Copyright © 2009 Wayland

Wayland
338 Euston Road
London NW1 3BH

Wayland
Level 17/207 Kent Street
Sydney NSW 2000

Editor: Victoria Brooker
Designer: Stephen Prosser

Brtish Cataloguing in Publication Data
 Green, Jen.
  The Yangtze. -- (Journey along a river)
  1. Yangtze River (China)--Juvenile literature. 2. Yangtze
  River Valley (China)--Juvenile literature
  I. Title II. Series
  915.1'2-dc22

 ISBN: 978 0 7502 5873 9

Printed in China

Wayland is a division of Hachette Children's Books,
an Hachette UK company.
www.hachette.co.uk

The website addresses (URLs) included in this book were valid at the time of going to press. However, because of the nature of the Internet, it is possible that some addresses may have changed, or sites may have changed or closed down since publication. While the author and Publisher regret any inconvenience this may cause readers, no responsibility for any such changes can be accepted by either the author or the Publisher.

The maps in this book use a conical projection, and so the indicator for North on the main map is only approximate.

Picture Acknowledgements

Cover: James Davis Travel Photography; title page Malcolm Watson/ Still Pictures; contents Chris Catton/ Oxford Scientific Films; 5 & 13 (bottom) James Davis Travel Photography; 6 Ian Cumming/Tibet Images; 7 Josef Müller, www.Open-Eye-Photography.de; 8 Philip Reeve/ Eye Ubiquitous; 9 (top) Julia Waterlow/ Eye Ubiquitous; 9 (bottom) Nick Bonetti/ Eye Ubiquitous; 10 Rhodri Jones/ Panos Pictures; 11 Julio Etchart/ Still Pictures; 12 (top) Michael S. Yamashita/Corbis (bottom) Popperfoto; 13 Martyn Evans/ Travel Ink; 14 Mark Henley/ Panos Pictures; 15 Mark Henley/ Panos PicturesPage 16 Nathan Smith/ Sylvia Cordaiy Photo Library; 17 David Lansdown/ Sylvia Cordaiy Photo Library; 18 Mark Henley/ Panos Pictures; 19 Camera Press; 20 Tony Binns/ Easi-er; 21 (top) Malcolm Watson/ Still Pictures (bottom) James Davis Worldwide Photographic Travel Library; 22/23 Mark Henley/ Panos Pictures; 24 (main) Guy Marks/ Axiom (inset) Liu Liqun/Corbis; 25 Liu Liqun/Corbis; 26 Bobby Yip/ Reuters/ Popperfoto; 27 (right) Jiri Rezac/ Axiom (bottom) Johnathan Smith/ Sylvia Cordaiy Photo Library; 28 & 29 Johnathan Smith/ Sylvia Cordaiy Photo; 30 Benoit Gysembergh/ Camera Press; 31 (top) Zhang dunhua-Imagine China (inset right) Bobby Yip/ Reuters/ Popperfoto; 32 Edward Parker; 33 (top) Stephen Coyne/ Sylvia Cordaiy Photo Library; 33 (inset) Julio Etchart/ Still Pictures (bottom) Alain le Garsmeur/ Panos Pictures; 34 N. Durrell McKenne/ Hutchinson Library; 35 Chris Catton/ Oxford Scientific Films; 36 Roland Seitre/ Still Pictures; 37 Tony Binns/Easi-er; 38 Richard Sharpley/ Hodder Wayland Picture Library; 39 (left) Tiziana and Gianni Baldizzone/Corbis (right) Gordon Clements/ Hodder Wayland Picture Library; 40 Robert Francis/ Hutchinson Library; 41 (left) Ric Ergenbright/Corbis (bottom) James Davis Worldwide Photographic Travel Library; 42 Catherine Platt/ Panos Pictures; 43 Earth Satellite Corporation/ Science Photo Library; 44/45 Mark Henley/ Impact

Contents

Words in **bold** can be found in the glossary on page 47.

Your guide to the river

Using the maps

The map below shows the whole length of the river as it flows through China. The white squares show how our journey along the Yangtze has been divided into six stages.

The numbered boxes show where places of interest are found.

Map references

Each chapter has a map showing the part of the river we have reached.

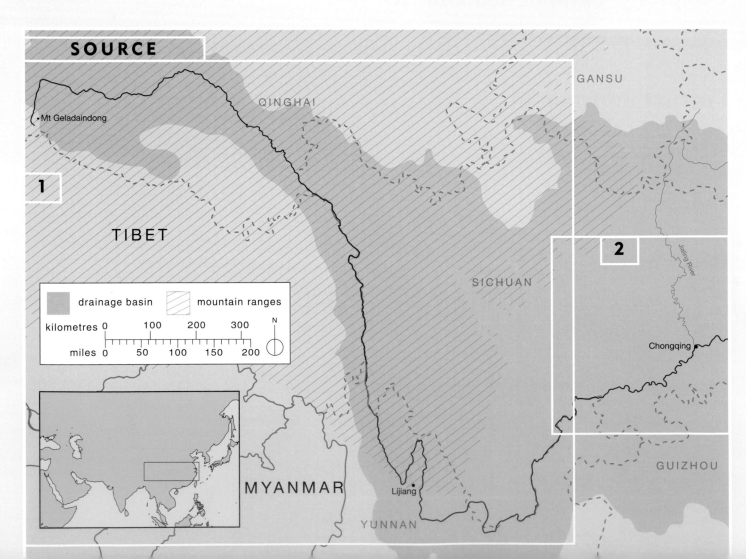

The journey ahead

The Yangtze is Asia's longest river. It flows for 6,300 kilometres. Its Chinese name, Chang Jiang, means the Long River. The river begins on a high plateau in western China. It drops down through steep valleys and over foaming **rapids**. It gets larger as other rivers join it. It flows through a wide valley near the city of Chongqing. Then it enters a dramatic gorge where the river has been dammed. This has affected the people who live there. Finally, the Yangtze wanders across a vast plain and empties into the East China Sea. We are following the river all the way from the mountains to the sea.

Our journey begins with a flight over the upper course of the Yangtze. We land at Lijiang, and then head on by road to an incredibly deep gorge.

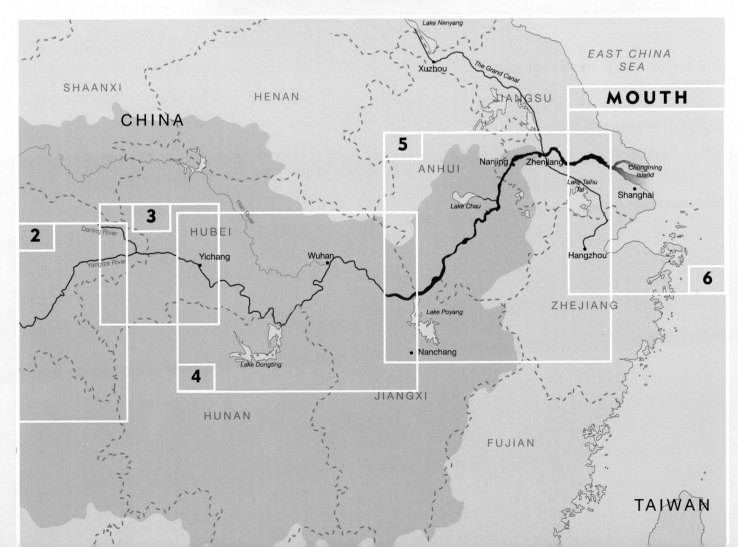

1. Mountains and gorges

The Yangtze begins on the high Qinghai-Tibet Plateau. As we fly over the plateau we see how vast and remote this region is. We will follow the Yangtze for about 1,400 kilometres as it plunges down through deep mountain valleys. Then we will land at Lijiang and catch a bus to the spectacular Tiger Leaping Gorge. We will find out about farming in the region. There will be time to learn about the people of Lijiang before we move on.

▼ **People keep herds of yaks on the Tibetan plateau. Yaks have thick hair to keep out the cold in winter.**

Mt Geladaindong

QINGHAI

TIBET

Yangtze River

SICHUAN

INDIA

km 0   100   200
miles 0   50   100   150

MYANMAR

Lijiang

YUNNAN

► **People need wood for fuel. But cutting down trees speeds up erosion.**

Mysterious source

The place where a river starts is called the **source**. Finding the source of a river like the Yangtze is not easy, because so many streams and rivers join it. For many years, people thought a river called the Jinsha Jiang was the source. 'Jiang' means 'river' in Chinese. Then in 1976, a small lake called Qemo Lake was discovered at the foot of mighty Mount Geladaindong. This remote mountain is 6,559 metres high. People now think this lake, fed by a **glacier**, is the source.

Fragile soil

Spring and summer are the rainy season along the upper Yangtze. Storms are common at this time. Rainwater pours down the steep slopes, wearing away the soil. This is called **erosion**.

Erosion is now happening more quickly because of people's actions. Local people cut down trees to burn as fuel and also use for building. Their animals strip the ground bare of plants. This is called overgrazing. But without trees and plant roots to hold the soil in place, it wears away more quickly.

Slowing erosion

Erosion has become a serious problem in the region. In 2001, the Chinese government launched an action plan to try to slow it down. Local people have been taught about the causes of erosion, including cutting down trees and overgrazing. New laws are helping to prevent further damage to the land.

Tourism comes to Lijiang

After tracing the course of the Upper Yangtze our plane lands at Lijiang. The airport here opened in 1994. It has brought money and new opportunities to the region. Tourism has become big business. Lijiang is an old city with narrow streets and a unique way of life. It is now a major tourist attraction. The town is also the starting point for a trip to Tiger Leaping Gorge MAP REF 1.

We take a bus ride to the gorge along a narrow road cut into the mountainside. Only a low wall protects us from a

▲ **Few people live along the Upper Yangtze. We spot these small villages from our plane.**

sheer 200-metre drop into the valley far below! This road was finished in 1997 as part of a plan to bring tourism to the region.

We leave the bus and **descend** 1,000 steps to a viewpoint above the river. The path is lined with stalls selling refreshments and souvenirs. You can even arrange for porters to carry you back up in a **sedan** chair – but spare a thought for the porters!

Tiger Leaping Gorge

Tiger Leaping Gorge is an amazing place. The river squeezes through a narrow gorge and tumbles over rapids. Sheer rock walls tower up to 3,000 metres high on either side. This is one of the world's deepest gorges. It has been carved by the tremendous force of the rushing water.

The Yangtze falls a total of 300 metres as it plunges over eighteen sets of rapids here. Rapids form where a river crosses a band of hard rocks. The hard rocks wear away quite slowly. One of the very hardest rocks, Tiger Leaping Stone, perches above a place where the river is just 30 metres wide. A legend tells how a tiger leapt the foaming water here to escape from hunters. That's how the gorge got its name.

▶ **Tiger Leaping Gorge attracts many visitors.**

▼ **The Yangtze crashes past tourists at Tiger Leaping Stone.**

Mountain farms

We leave Tiger Leaping Gorge and head back towards Lijiang. Much of the countryside around here is farmed, but there is little flat land. Farmers cut steps into steep hillsides to make small fields. The steps are called **terraces**.

Stone walls support the terraces. This helps to prevent the soil from washing away in a downpour. Farmers also cut little ditches to channel water from streams into their fields. Much of the farm work here is done by hand. But water buffalo are used to plough the larger fields before planting.

Different crops

Many different crops grow here. Farmers grow maize, potatoes and rice to feed their families. This type of farming is called **subsistence farming**.

▼ **A farmer begins to terrace steep ground. You can see more terraces in the background.**

Sunflowers, tobacco and oilseed rape are grown to sell. Crops grown for sale are called **cash crops**.

Flood danger

Cutting down trees is very destructive. When trees are removed, heavy rain can wash the soil into the river. This adds to the **sediment** which is already in the river. The channel becomes shallow, so the river holds less water. This makes flooding more likely.

Since the 1950s half of all the forests along the Yangtze have been cut down. Scientists warned that this could lead to flooding, but the government did

▲ **Erosion happens quickly when trees are removed. Sometimes the whole hillside slips away in a landslide.**

not listen. In 1998, the scientists' fears came true. The river burst its banks after heavy rain, causing the worst flooding in nearly fifty years. The government finally acted to prevent more damage.

Taking action

Strict new laws were passed to reduce tree cutting. Local people were told about the dangers of tree cutting. In the worst-affected areas, trees have now been planted to slow down the rate of erosion.

▲ The Naxi orchestra is centuries old.

◄ This holy man is writing in Naxi script. This writing is a series of pictures, not letters.

The Naxi of Lijiang

We return to Lijiang to meet a people called the Naxi. They were originally from Tibet but have lived around Lijiang for over a thousand years. The Naxi live by farming and herding. They grow rice and wheat, and also breed strong horses.

In recent years the Naxi have also earned money through tourism. People come to find out about Naxi culture.

The Naxi follow a religion called Dongba. They believe that all natural things have soul. They worship natural forces such as the sun and moon, clouds and mountains, and of course, the mighty Yangtze.

▲ **These men are rebuilding houses destroyed in the earthquake. Money from tourism helps pay for this work.**

Writing and music

Dongba scholars are translating ancient writings from the tenth century. Their writing is very unusual. The Naxi are the last people in the world who write using pictures, not letters.

Music also plays a big part in Naxi culture. In Lijiang we enjoy a performance by the famous Naxi orchestra. This orchestra is said to date back to the thirteenth century. The great emperor Kublai Khan gave instruments to the Naxi after they helped his army to cross the river. The instruments are either strummed or struck to produce beautiful, haunting sounds.

Rebuilding Lijiang

In 1996 a major **earthquake** struck the Lijiang area. Over 250 people died and thousands more were injured. About a third of Lijiang was destroyed, including many old buildings.

Lijiang is now being rebuilt. The Chinese government is also developing the city as a centre for tourism. It hopes the spectacular Yangtze gorges and Naxi culture will bring tourists to the region.

We take off from Lijiang and follow the river. We land in Chongqing where we can take to the river at last!

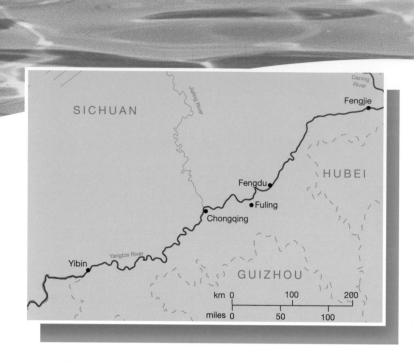

2. The Sichuan basin

When we land in Chongqing, we have already followed the Yangtze for over half of its journey. We explore this bustling city and sample the local cooking. The river is central to Chongqing's economy and to trade in the region. As we continue our journey, we reach part of the river that has been transformed by a huge **dam**. This has affected the lives of local people.

▼ **Chongqing is growing fast. This view is from a cable car that crosses the river.**

▲ People balance heavy loads on their shoulders as they descend the steep path to Chaotianmen Docks.

Rivers join

At Chongqing we see a major change in the Yangtze. The river is much wider and slower here. Several minor rivers, called **tributaries**, have already joined the Yangtze. At Chongqing another river, the Jialing, joins it from the north.

The place where two rivers meet is called a **confluence**. Chongqing grew up on a narrow neck of land between the two rivers. But it has now spread to the mainland on both sides. Cable cars have been built to carry people across the rivers to the mainland. You get fantastic views of the city from these cable cars.

Crowded streets

Chongqing is the largest city in south-west China. Over six million people live here. Another 24 million people live in the surrounding area. For years the city was governed as part of Sichuan Province. But in 1997 Chongqing became self-governing – a sign of its importance.

With so many people, the streets are crowded, especially near the docks. These streets are too steep for bicycles, which are used to carry loads in other parts of China. People sling heavy weights from poles balanced across their shoulders. It takes a lot of skill to balance the loads as you move through narrow streets and climb steep steps.

▲ Chongqing is a centre for the car industry. The finished vehicles are transported by barge.

Centre of industry

The area around Chongqing is rich in minerals. Mercury, manganese and rock salt are found here. Coal and natural gas are also mined. These minerals and the city's location on the river make it an ideal base for industry.

Chaotianmen Docks are a bustling centre of activity. From here, millions of tonnes of cargo travel upriver, or downstream as far as the ocean. Goods also reach other parts of China by road and rail.

Manufacturing

Since the 1980s, Chongqing has been an important centre for manufacturing. Cars and motorbikes are made here. By 2007, Chongqing's factories were producing about a million cars and over eight million motorbikes a year!

Chongqing's thriving industries have caused it to grow quickly. Huge cranes dot the city, marking building sites. Each new building seems to tower higher than the last. However, industrial success has a downside. Waste gases from factories and traffic cause **air pollution**. Chongqing is permanently swathed in a dirty haze called **smog**. Pollution also affects the river, as we will soon find out.

What's cooking?

Before leaving Chongqing we sample the local cooking. Many local dishes are hot and spicy, as they are cooked with chilli pepper. Chicken, pork, duck and fish are all on the menu. There are more unusual dishes too – stewed frog and snake!

Sichuan hotpot is a famous local dish. People cook their own meat and vegetables at the table, in a bubbling pot of chicken stock. The cooked food is flavoured with spicy oil, salt and chilli.

Hotpot was invented in Chongqing. You can try it in most cafés, which also have outdoor tables. Cafés are great places to meet people and watch the world go by!

▼ **Sichuan hotpot is a local speciality. Cooking food at the table is fun!**

A changed landscape

A **funicular railway** carries us down to the river. There we board a passenger ferry which carries us downstream towards Fengjie.

This stretch of the river has been completely transformed by the building of a huge dam downriver. The Three Gorges Dam lies at Sandouping. Later in our journey we will visit it. But it is this part of the river that the dam has changed the most.

Rising waters

The Three Gorges Project was completed in 2008. As soon as it was finished, water started to build up behind the dam. The water level rose slowly and a long, narrow lake called a **reservoir** formed.

By 2009, the entire river valley between Chongqing and Sandouping was flooded. Low-lying land by the river was covered by the world's largest reservoir, stretching for 630 kilometres.

◀ **This picture of a pagoda by the Yangtze was taken before 2008. The water later rose to cover the houses below the temple.**

Moving home

The Three Gorges Dam has changed this stretch of the river forever. The water level rose by up to 100 metres directly behind the dam. The rising water not only flooded farmland, it also covered 19 cities, 326 towns and 1,300 villages. Many historic sites were lost.

To make way for the reservoir, people in all these settlements had to move – over 1.2 million people in all. This was the one of the largest resettlements that has ever taken place anywhere. The move took between 1997 and 2009.

In some areas, such as Chongqing, people only had to move to higher ground. In other places, whole villages and towns had to be relocated far from the river.

People received money for the government to help with the move. But many were still unhappy about leaving their homes, where their families had lived for generations.

▶ **These villagers are moving all their possessions. Many people were unhappy about the move.**

The 'Golden Waterway'

The Yangtze is the most important waterway in China. Eighty per cent of the total cargo transported on China's rivers goes via this river. For this reason the Yangtze is called the 'Golden Waterway'.

The stretch of river we are travelling now, between Chongqing and Yichang, used to be too shallow for large ships to **navigate**. **Deposits** of sand and gravel called shoals were a hazard to shipping. However, those **shoals** are now a thing of the past. The new reservoir has increased the water depth dramatically.

Large ocean-going vessels are now able to travel all the way from the East China Sea to Chongqing. We watch one passing now, across the wide reservoir. There are now many more boats on the river.

A dirty river

Increased river traffic has brought wealth to cities along the river, such as Chongqing, and Fuling downstream. We call at the port of Fuling and head on towards Fengdu. The Yangtze is vital

▼ **Boats up to ten times this size can now travel the Yangtze thanks to the Three Gorges Dam.**

to China's economy. However, the industries along the banks cause a lot of pollution. The steel and chemical factories we are passing produce huge amounts of waste. Farming also causes pollution when the chemicals farmers use on their fields end up in the river.

In 2002, a study reported that over six million tonnes of rubbish were dumped in the Upper Yangtze each year –

▲ **Cities along the banks of the Yangtze produce huge amounts of domestic waste.**

along with almost ten million tonnes of solid waste from industry. Huge amounts of liquid waste from homes, sewage and industry also end up here. The government launched a major effort to clean up the Yangtze. It pledged to spend US$4.8 billion on waste control between 2002 and 2012.

Our ferry arrives at Fengjie. We transfer to a cruise boat and head towards the Three Gorges.

3. The Three Gorges

Fengjie is a busy town at the gateway to the famous Three Gorges region. We join tourists on a cruise boat and head downstream. We explore the amazing Three Gorges. These sights have been altered by the building of the enormous Three Gorges Dam, but they are still breathtaking. We head downriver to reach the huge dam itself at Sandouping. We then continue downstream towards Yichang, passing the smaller Gezhou Dam on the way.

▼ **The beauty and huge scale of the Qutang Gorge has amazed travellers for centuries.**

Stunning gorges

The Three Gorges are one of the most famous sights in China. These limestone gorges stretch for 130 kilometres. They were carved by water around 70 million years ago. A huge inland sea wore away the rock along deep cracks in the Earth's surface.

In places, the gorge walls rise to jagged peaks towering 1,200 metres above us. Elsewhere, the water has carved weird shapes in the soft rock.

A changing landscape

As the Yangtze passes through the gorges, several small tributaries join it. In places these small rivers have cut deep **ravines**. As erosion continues, these ravines will gradually deepen, and may eventually become gorges, too.

However, some of the smaller tributaries are now covered by water. The water level here is now much higher than it was before the enormous dam was built downstream.

Gorge cruises

Most visitors see the Three Gorges from the deck of a cruise boat, as we are doing now. Some of these cruise boats are very luxurious. By 2020 China is expected to become one of the world's top tourist destinations. The Three Gorges will be one of the main attractions. Several tour companies have ordered new boats to carry tourists.

The Qutang Gorge

The first gorge heading downstream is Qutang Gorge MAP REF 1. It is only eight kilometres long but very spectacular, with almost vertical walls.

At the end of the Qutang Gorge we dock at Wushan. We take a side trip along the Daning River to visit the Lesser Three Gorges MAP REF 2. They may be lesser by name, but many people think they are even more stunning than the main gorges.

Yangtze dragons

Back on the Yangtze we head down to Wu Gorge MAP REF 3. This gorge is famous for its dragons! An ancient legend says twelve wild dragons made havoc here, causing floods and destruction.

Yao Ji, daughter of the Queen Mother of the West, defeated the dragons. She and her eleven sisters turned into twelve peaks – six on each side of the gorge. As we pass through the gorge we spot

◀ **Tourists watch as their cruise boat approaches the Qutang Gorge.**

◀ **Some cruise boats carry over 250 passengers. These large boats are like floating hotels.**

▶ **Legends surround the peaks lining the Wu Gorge.**

Goddess Peak. This is said to be Yao Ji herself in the shape of a kneeling girl.

Beware of rocks

We reach the last gorge, Xiling MAP REF 4. This is the longest gorge, 76 kilometres long. In the past it was also the most dangerous. Many travellers drowned in its rough waters, dotted with rocks.

In the 1950s, the government improved navigation here by blasting away the dangerous rocks with dynamite. The gorge is now much safer. But boats still keep between markers that show the safest route.

A new Great Wall

The Great Wall of China is the country's most famous landmark. But now there is another Great Wall – the Three Gorges Dam! The dam comes into sight as we leave the Xiling Gorge. It lies at the town of Sandouping MAP REF 5.

This new Great Wall is huge. It stretches two kilometres across the river, and towers 185 metres high. We bypass this enormous barrier using a series of four locks to the side.

▼ **When fully working in 2012, the Three Gorges Dam will provide ten per cent of China's electricity.**

For and against

The dam has caused a lot of argument. One of its main purposes is to **generate** electricity. The dam is part of a huge power station that produces electricity from fast-flowing water. This is called **hydroelectricity**. The Three Gorges Dam is the largest hydroelectric plant in the world.

The dam also has several other uses. Its supporters say it will also improve navigation and control floods. The Yangtze has a history of bad flooding. In the twentieth century alone, floods killed 320,000 people here.

▶ **Some 30,000 workers, 40 cranes and hundreds of trucks helped to build the Three Gorges Dam. It was China's largest building project since the Great Wall.**

Other people were against the dam. They said it would damage the environment, and 1.2 million people had to move to make way for it. They said a series of smaller dams would have done less damage. However, the dam's supporters won the argument, and work began in 1994. The project was completed in 2008.

Trapping sediment

The Yangtze carries about 600 million tonnes of sediment downstream every year. Some experts fear the dam will trap sediment, which will then build up upstream. This could make the **channel** shallower, causing problems for ships. It would also increase the risk of flooding in the region.

Engineers have built 23 **sluice gates** into the dam to wash sediment downstream. But no one is quite sure yet if they will work properly.

Our route downriver is blocked by another dam – the Gezhou Dam. We pass using a ship lock.

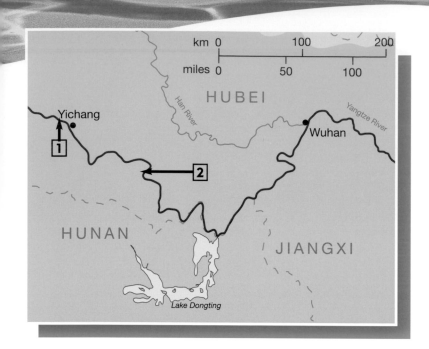

4. The Yangtze plains

We pass the Gezhou Dam and dock at Yichang. Here we board a passenger ferry and continue downstream. The Yangtze flows more slowly now, and starts to weave through a vast, flat plain. Flooding is a major danger here. We take a side trip to Lake Dongting, China's second-largest lake. Later we visit a textile factory in the city of Wuhan.

▼ **The landscape beyond Yichang is fairly flat. The river curves around enormous bends.**

Ship-locks

The Gezhou Dam MAP REF 1 is 2.6 kilometres wide and 70 metres high. We pass the dam by entering a ship lock. These locks lower or raise ships so they can pass to different levels on the river.

As we enter the lock, the water level is the same as in the river behind the dam. The enormous doors close behind us. As water in the dock is let out, the level starts to drop. In about an hour we reach the level of the river below the dam. The doors open and we sail out. These locks are vital to navigation along the Yangtze.

▲ **Cruise boats in the ship-lock at the Gezhou Dam.**

Winding through the plain

We leave our cruise boat at Yichang, and continue by ferry. Now the landscape becomes much flatter. For thousands of years, the Yangtze has spread sediment over this area in times of flood. This has gradually formed a vast fertile plain called a **floodplain**.

The river is moving slowly now. It wanders across the plain in a series of huge loops called **meanders**. In places, the river eventually cuts through the neck of one of the loops. A small crescent-shaped lake is left behind.

Risk of floods

The floodplain through which we are passing is very fertile because of all the sediment dropped by the river when it floods. This land is good for farming and is also densely populated. However, the whole vast area is at risk of flooding. People fight a constant battle to keep the river at bay. In 1998, the Yangtze burst its banks and flooded 197,000 hectares of land. That's about the same as 280,000 football pitches.

One way to prevent flooding is to build high earth walls called **levees** along the river to contain the water. One major levee, the Jingjiang Levee MAP REF 2 is 182 kilometres long. It was started in AD 345 – 1,665 years ago! It now protects eight million people, two major cities, and 800,000 hectares of farmland.

As we journey down the Yangtze we will see many more levees. In fact there are over 3,600 kilometres of major levees and 30,000 kilometres of smaller ones!

▼ **Floodplains provide good farmland. But a severe flood can destroy crops and livestock.**

▲ **The army and volunteers try to mend a levee which burst during the floods in 1998.**

▶ **People used boats in the streets of Jiujiang during the flood.**

Drastic action

Levees are built to protect people and land. But if a levee gives way during a severe flood, it can make the situation worse. A wall of water surges over the bank and washes over the land. During the 1998 floods, several levees gave way and caused massive damage. Water entered the city of Jiujiang beyond Wuhan, and flooded 40,000 homes.

To avoid similar danger elsewhere, the government took drastic action. It removed 330,000 people from their

homes along the Upper Yangtze. The area was then allowed to flood. This was done to reduce the risk of flooding in large cities and industrial areas downstream.

Lake Dongting

Beyond the Jingjiang Levee we reach Lake Dongting, China's second-biggest lake. It covers 2,740 kilometres – that's an area nearly twice the size of London!

However, 150 years ago Lake Dongting was even bigger – twice its present size. What has happened? As the Yangtze reaches the lake, the water spreads out and slows down. The lazy **current** drops sediment, which has caused the lake to **silt** up.

Local farmers have built little banks to reclaim land at the water's edge for farming. But the government has said this land is needed to store water when the Yangtze is running high. The swampy shore helps to prevent flooding.

Transport links

We sail on to reach Wuhan. Here the Yangtze is joined by its largest tributary, the Han River. The Han is 1,540 kilometres long and flows from the north-west. Wuhan is a major port and lies at the heart of a transport network. From here, roads and railways as well as rivers spread out in many directions. The docks, streets and railway station are busy with traffic.

▼ **This land on the shores of Lake Dongting has been reclaimed for farming.**

▲ This bridge carries both a road and a railway line.

▶ Thousands of women work in Wuhan's clothes factories.

The Yangtze is 1,500 metres wide here. At one time the only way to cross the river was by ferry. But in 1957 the Changjiang Bridge was built to carry road and rail traffic.

Textile industry

Wuhan is an industrial city, with iron and steel works. Cars and ships are also built here. But the most important industry is textiles. Wuhan lies close to one of China's main cotton-growing areas. Its factories **export** clothes and textiles all over the world.

China is one of the world's top producers of clothing. Perhaps you are wearing something made in China? If so, it may have come all the way from Wuhan!

We leave Wuhan on a grain barge. We head into an important farming region.

5. Land of fish and rice

Beyond Wuhan we enter the 'land of fish and rice'. As this name suggests, farming and fishing are both very important here. The Lower Yangtze produces about 70 per cent of China's **paddy rice** and over half of its freshwater fish. We visit the ancient capital of Nanjing. Then we head on to the city of Zhenjiang where the Grand Canal meets the Yangtze.

▼ **This farmer is feeding fish kept in a pond. This practice is called fish farming.**

Fishing

Fishing is an important industry along this part of the Yangtze and in nearby lakes. China catches more freshwater fish than any other nation and over half of it comes from the Yangtze!

Various fishing methods are used on the river. The most unusual one involves the use of tame cormorants. These birds are expert fish-catchers. They dive from small fishing boats to catch fish underwater. But they can't swallow the fish because of a ring around their necks. They bring the catch back to the boat and get a fish reward when they finish work. We will get a chance to try the local fish dishes on our journey.

▲ **These fishermen are working with cormorants. This is an ancient method which still works today!**

Fish farming

China leads the world in fish farming. In 2005 it produced over 32 million tonnes of farmed fish, more than any other nation. Some of this fish is sold abroad, but a lot gets eaten in China.

Farmers rear fish in ponds on their land. These ponds have other uses too. They supply water for crops, and their sediment is used as fertiliser. Farm waste is put into the pond to encourage the growth of weeds that feed the fish. This simple but efficient system has been used for about 5,000 years!

Threatened wildlife

Today, wild fish and other river creatures are in danger. This is partly because there is so much fishing, but river traffic and pollution are also to blame. Falling numbers of fish caused fish catches to drop steeply in the twentieth century. In 1954, 434,000 tonnes of fish were caught. By 2002 this figure was less than 100,000 tonnes.

To protect river fish the government has banned **commercial** fishing between February and May. This is when most of the rare fish breed.

▲ **The beautiful Yangtze dolphin is now probably extinct.**

Rare mammal

The rarest species in the Yangtze is the baiji, or river dolphin. This unique animal has lived in the river for over 70 million years. However, in the last century many baijis died after getting caught in fishing nets or being hit by boats. In 1950 there were about 6,000 baijis living in the Yangtze. Recently scientists searched for baiji in vain. This animal is now probably extinct. If not, it is one of the world's very rarest mammals.

Irrigation

Quite a lot of the land around us is artificially watered using water drawn from rivers and lakes. This practice is called **irrigation**. Chinese farmers have been doing this for 4,000 years!

Some of the irrigation methods used have hardly changed in all that time. We see waterwheels and other simple devices to raise water in the fields

▼ **A farmer uses a simple machine to raise water. You can also see an old waterwheel, traditionally used to raise water.**

around us as we travel down the Yangtze. Farmers dig little ditches to channel river water into their fields. Electric and petrol-driven pumps are also used to raise river water. Between 1950 and 2000, the area of irrigated land trebled, to an amazing 51 million hectares. This is over half of all China's farmland.

As the demand for food increases, so irrigation will expand too. By 2050 the amount of irrigated land in China may be greater than the size of the UK and Japan combined!

▲ **A farmer transplants seedlings into the paddy field. His wide hat protects him from the sun.**

Rice growing

Rice is the main food crop in China. Almost everyone eats it every day. Two types of rice are grown – upland rice and wet paddy rice. The wet rice is grown in flooded fields called paddies. Rainfall provides some water for the paddies, but most comes from irrigation. Water is raised or pumped from streams and rivers and channelled into the fields.

China produces about a third of the world's wet rice. You can see rice growing in paddies all around us. Warm weather and plentiful water makes this area ideal for rice-growing. In fact it is called 'the rice bowl of China'.

A tough life

Growing rice is very hard work. The method of farming has hardly changed in 2,000 years. The first step is to sow the rice seedlings in a nursery field. After four to five weeks the **seedlings** are replanted in a flooded paddy.

Small walls are built around the plot to contain water. Farmers gradually increase the water depth as the rice grows. They also weed the plot and may add chemicals to control insect pests. After ten to twelve weeks the rice turns golden. It is now ready for harvest. The farmer breaks down the walls to drain the paddy before the rice harvest can begin again.

▲ Most Chinese people eat rice at least once a day.

▶ Chinese farmers grow vegetables to sell at market.

Rice harvest

The whole family helps to harvest, **thresh** and store the rice. Finally, a water buffalo is used to plough the plot, ready for a new crop. Some farmers grow two rice crops in a year. They also grow wheat and other crops, usually in winter.

Southern capital

We now approach the ancient city of Nanjing. Nanjing means 'southern capital'. Sure enough, Nanjing has been China's capital for long periods in history. It was founded in the fifth century BCE. Over the centuries it was the capital of no less than ten kingdoms – or **dynasties** as they are called in China. It was also the capital of the Republic of China from 1911 to 1949. Then the capital was moved to Beijing.

Nanjing's city walls come into view. These were originally built about 2,500 years ago. The present walls date back to 1369. They stretch for 32 kilometres around the city, and are the longest city walls in the world!

Nanjing attracts tourists from other parts of China and abroad. Most come to see the walls. People also visit the burial place of Sun Yat-sen, who founded modern China in 1911.

▼ **The burial place of Sun Yat-sen is a tourist attraction.**

The Grand Canal

About 80 kilometres beyond Nanjing we reach another great waterway, the Grand Canal. This crosses the Yangtze at Zhenjiang MAP REF 1. It runs between Beijing in the north and Hangzhou in the south. At 1,800 kilometres long, it is the world's longest waterway. The canal was started 2,400 years ago!

The canal is still used to transport cargo such as grain. We leave our grain barge, which heads up the canal.

At present barges cannot travel the whole length of the canal because parts are silted up. Engineers plan to **divert** water from the Yangtze to raise the level of the canal. The worst sections will be **dredged**, which should solve the problem. The government also plans to extend the canal south of Hangzhou to the port of Ningbo.

◀ **Barges travel nose to tail up the Grand Canal, like a gigantic water serpent!**

We board another passenger ferry for the last part of our journey. We head for the great port of Shanghai.

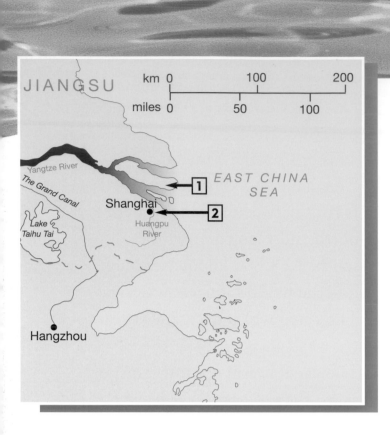

JIANGSU

km 0   100   200
miles 0   50   100

Yangtze River

The Grand Canal

Lake
Taihu Tai

Shanghai

Huangpu
River

EAST CHINA
SEA

1

2

Hangzhou

▼ **The busy streets of Shanghai. Shanghai is one of the world's biggest cities, with over 20 million people.**

6. The Yangtze delta

We enter the vast Yangtze delta. Here the river slows and widens as it approaches the sea. The delta has long been important for trade. Shanghai, one of China's biggest cities, lies at the mouth of the Yangtze. China's economy is growing quickly, and Shanghai is playing a key role in this process. We explore the city that marks our journey's end.

Watery world

A delta forms where a river slows as it reaches the sea, and drops sediment. Over millions of years sediment has built up here to form a huge flat area. Streams and channels criss-cross the delta as water finds its way to the sea.

The Yangtze widens to about 80 kilometres across at the mouth. A large island called Chongming Island lies here MAP REF 1. It is made of sediment. The island splits the Yangtze in two. We follow the southern channel towards the city of Shanghai.

A teeming city

The Yangtze delta is one of the most densely **populated** parts of China. An average of 2,700 people live in each square kilometre of Shanghai. That compares to just 140 people per square kilometre in China as a whole. Some parts of the city are even more crowded, with an incredible 50,000 people per

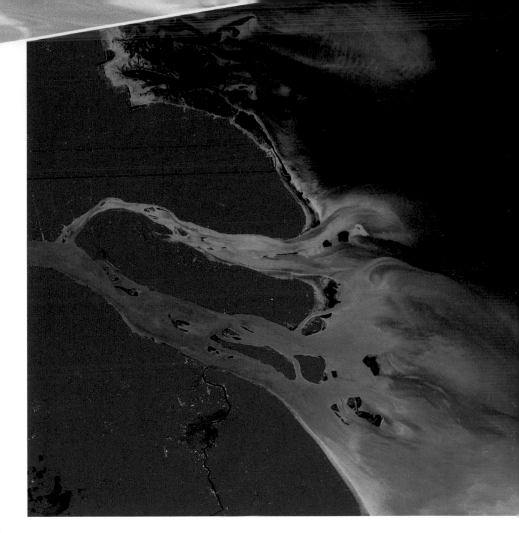

▲ **This false-colour photo taken by a satellite shows Chongming Island in the middle of the Yangtze.**

square kilometre, living in skyscrapers! Shanghai is so crowded that every spare bit of land has been built on. Housing is now spreading beyond the suburbs onto neighbouring farmland. However, this reduces the amount of food that can be grown. Chinese architects plan to solve the problem of space by building more giant skyscrapers. If there is no room to spread outwards, the only way to build is up!

A new district

We leave our ferry at the port of Shanghai. We head towards the city centre up the Huangpu River. We get off at Shiliupu Wharf and stroll along the Bund, the main street on the west bank of the Huangpu. The Bund is lined with old buildings that date from colonial times.

Across the river in the special economic zone of Pudong MAP REF 2 . This new commercial district is an example of China's fast economic growth.

In 1990, Pudong was little more than farmland. Since then it has rapidly developed into a huge, thriving business centre. It now covers over 100 square kilometres! Computers and all sorts of high-tech equipment are made here.

Links with the world

The Huangpu River links Pudong to the Yangtze and the East China Sea. Goods made in Pudong and other parts of

China leave the docks here bound for ports around the world. The southern channel of the Yangtze has recently been dredged to make it easier for large ships to dock here. Shanghai and Pudong prove that the Yangtze is still central to China's economy.

◄ The television tower dominates the landscape of Pudong. It also marks the end of our journey!

Journey's end

Our journey is now over. Our flight home leaves from Pudong International Airport, which opened in 1999. From the airport we look out at the point where the Yangtze meets the sea. It's been an incredible journey. We've seen 6,300 kilometres of amazing landscapes. We've also learned about the people who live along the river. It's no wonder the Chinese are proud of their great river, the Yangtze.

The Yangtze drops thousands of metres on the first half of its 6,300-kilometre journey. The second half is much flatter.

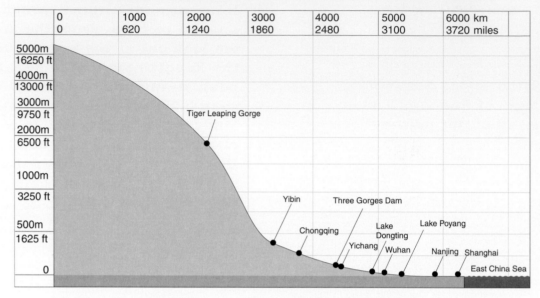

Further information

Useful websites

These websites discuss the Three Gorges Dam on the Yangtze:
http://www.pbs.org/itvs/greatwall/
See also
http://www.africanwater.org/yangtze.htm

Center for Global Education web page has facts about the Yangtze, its landscapes and people:
cgee.hamline.edu/rivers/Resources/river_profiles/Yangtze.html

China Culture website about the scenic wonders of the Yangtze:
http://www.culturalink.gov.cn/gb/en_travel/2003-09/24/content_34069.htm

Books

Changing Face of China by Stephen Keeler (Wayland, 2007)

Changing World: China by Jen Green (Franklin Watts, 2008)

Fact at your Fingertips: Asia by Derek Hall (Wayland, 2008)

Food and Celebrations: China by Sylvia Goulding (Wayland, 2008)

Geography Now: Rivers Around the World by Jen Green (Wayland, 2008)

Geography Detective: Rivers by Jen Green (Wayland, 2006)

Glossary

basin the area drained by a river and its tributaries.

canal an artificial waterway.

cash crops crops that are grown for sale.

channel the passage through which a river flows, or to direct water a certain way.

commercial of something that is done for trade or profit.

confluence a place where rivers meet.

current a regular flow of water in a certain direction.

dam a barrier that diverts or holds back water.

delta a flat, swampy area that forms as a river drops sediment at its mouth.

deposit when something is left behind.

descend to go down.

divert to change the direction of something.

dredge to deepen a river so that ships can use it.

dynasty a series of rulers from the same family.

earthquake when rocks shift and crack because of enormous pressure below ground.

erosion when rocks and soil are worn away by rain, wind or ice.

export to sell a product abroad, or a product that is sold abroad.

floodplain the flattish land on either side of a river which floods after heavy rain.

funicular railway a railway with carriages pulled by a cable and pulley system.

generate to produce electricity.

glacier a mass of ice that flows slowly downhill.

gorge a deep, narrow valley with sheer sides.

hydroelectricity electricity that is made using fast-flowing water.

irrigation when farmers water their fields using water channelled from a river.

levee a wall made of earth to prevent flooding

location a place

lock an enclosed section of a river where the water level can be lowered or raised.

meander a looping bend on a river.

navigation the passage of ships and boats.

paddy rice the rice that is grown in paddy fields.

pagoda a temple in the form of a tower with many storeys.

pollution when the air, water or soil is harmed by a substance that doesn't belong there.

population the number of people living in an area.

rapids an area of rough water where a river crashes over rocks.

ravine a deep gorge.

reservoir an artificial lake used to store water, made by damming a river or stream.

sedan chair an enclosed chair fixed to two poles, and carried by porters.

sediment soil or small stones carried along by a river.

seedling a young plant.

shoal an underwater sandbank.

silt up when a river becomes clogged with sediment.

sluice gate a gate that controls the flow of water in a river or canal.

smog a dirty haze caused by air pollution.

source the place where a river begins.

subsistence farming when farmers grow food for their own families, with any extra sold at market.

terrace a step cut into a hillside to make a field.

thresh when a crop is beaten to separate the waste from the grain.

tributary a minor river or stream that joins the main river.

Index

Journey Along a River

Contents of titles in the series:

WAYLAND